SCALES AND ARPEGGIOS FOR CLASSICAL BANJO

MB21701

BY JOHN BULLARD

© 2009 BY MEL BAY PUBLICATIONS, INC., PACIFIC, MO 63069.
ALL RIGHTS RESERVED. INTERNATIONAL COPYRIGHT SECURED. B.M.I. MADE AND PRINTED IN U.S.A.
No part of this publication may be reproduced in whole or in part, or stored in a retrieval system, or transmitted in any form
or by any means, electronic, mechanical, photocopy, recording, or otherwise, without written permission of the publisher.

Visit us on the Web at www.melbay.com or billsmusicshelf.com

Acknowledgments

I would like to thank John Patykula for his undying support of my endeavors as a classical banjoist. John has been and continues to be a valued teacher, mentor, musical cohort and friend. He has contributed greatly to the conceptual and technical aspects of this book. Without John's guidance this project would not have been accomplished.

I would also like to thank James Wiznerowicz, DMA for his assistance in both the technical and conceptual realms of this book. James was key in my learning how this information could be best presented. James is Coordinator of Musicianship Studies and Associate Professor of Music at Virginia Commonwealth University.

Finally, I would like to thank Roland Karnatz for his editing skills and ample guidance. Roland's interest and encouragement has been invaluable.

Preface

This unique book of scales and arpeggios for the banjo by John Bullard covers all of the major and minor keys, presented in a clear and organized format. The serious student of any instrument should place a strong emphasis on the continuous study and practice of fundamental exercises, including scales and arpeggios. Scales and arpeggios are essential for the development of a secure technique, as well as being the foundation for all music theory. Through daily practice, the fingers will become more flexible and independent. In addition to training the fingers, practicing scales and arpeggios will help to train the ear to distinguish the various keys and intervals, allowing for a better understanding of the total scope of the instrument.

For many years, John Bullard has tried to elevate the banjo to the realm of other "serious" instruments through his numerous transcriptions and recordings, in particular the works of J.S. Bach. This book of scales and arpeggios is another important step towards the realization of that goal.

John Patykula
Associate Professor of Guitar
Virginia Commonwealth University

Table of Contents

About the Material	4
Special Considerations	6
Scales and Arpeggios	7
Continuous Exercise for Scales	21
Continuous Exercise for Arpeggios	27
Chromatic Scale Exercise	29
About the Author	31

About the Material
Use Standard G Tuning

1. Scales and Arpeggios

The scales and arpeggios are organized according to the circle of fifths, starting with G major and progressing through D, A, E, B, F sharp, D flat, A flat, E flat, B flat, F and ending with C major. G major is used as the starting point because it serves most easily as the home key for the banjo in G tuning. Each major scale is followed by the relative minor scales that share the same key signature (such as G major and E minor).

For each major key, the scales and arpeggios will be given in two octaves followed by the chordal cadences for that key. For the relative minor keys, both the melodic and harmonic minor scales will be given in two octaves along with the two octave arpeggio followed by the cadences for the minor key.

Exceptions to this pattern are the keys of C sharp minor and D flat major. These keys are limited to one octave on the standard 22 fret five-string banjo. For these keys, the scales and arpeggios will be given in one octave. The one octave versions will ascend to one note beyond the tonic to accommodate the rhythm of the exercise. This "extra" note will appear in parenthesis.

Some five-string banjos are made with varied scale lengths and have more than 22 frets (the Author's current banjo has a scale length of 25.5 inches and 23 frets). For this reason, Appendix A is included. This section contains two octave versions for the D flat major and C sharp minor scales and arpeggios, which are possible on a banjo with 23 or more frets. These two octave versions will use the same fingerings found on page 7.

Since the scales and arpeggios are in closed positions throughout (except for the few open strings found in D major and D minor), the fingerings that are given on the first page are to be followed throughout the remaining keys except where otherwise notated. In this way, the fingering patterns for G major and E minor found on page 7 serve as the fingering template throughout the material except where deviations are indicated for either the right or left hand pattern.

Left hand fingering is provided via the tablature staff as well as traditional fingering numbers found within the standard notation staff. In this system, the numbers 1, 2, 3 and 4 appearing in the standard notation staff represent the index, middle, ring and pinky fingers respectively.

Right hand fingering is given between the Tablature and standard notation staffs. T, i, m represent the thumb, index and middle fingers of the right hand.

On page seven, the scales are presented using a right hand pattern of alternating between the thumb and index fingers (T i T i ...etc.). This right hand pattern serves as a good starting point to use for learning and practicing the scales. Once this right hand pattern is fully mastered, other right hand patterns should be explored. Some examples would be alternating between the index and middle fingers (i m i m ...etc.) or between the middle and index fingers (m i m i ...etc.) or using three finger patterns such as thumb, index, middle (T i m T i m ...etc.) and so on.

2. Continuous Exercise for Scales

The continuous exercise for scales represents an example of how to practice the scales in one flowing, musical routine without stopping after each scale. This should be done only when all of the scales are fully mastered and memorized. This exercise goes through all of the scales (without the arpeggios or cadences) in the same order as previously presented. Each scale is connected by a two or four note figure, which leads into the next scale. The left hand fingering for these connective passages is given each time while the fingering for the scales themselves remains the same as found on page 7. The right hand fingering pattern given for this exercise is a constant alternation of the thumb and index fingers. Once this pattern is mastered, other right hand combinations can be employed.

3. Continuous Exercise for Arpeggios

The continuous exercise for arpeggios is the same concept as the previous exercise but utilizes the arpeggios alone. This exercise is an example of how to practice the arpeggios in a continuous musical format without stopping between each one. As with the scales, this should only be done once the arpeggios themselves are fully mastered and memorized. The arpeggios are given in a triplet rhythm with a triplet figure connecting each arpeggio. The left hand fingering for the arpeggios should be the same as found on page 7 and the fingering for each connective passage is provided. The right hand fingering for this exercise is given for the G major and E minor arpeggios and repeats this same pattern throughout.

4. Chromatic Scale Exercise

A chromatic scale includes every note, ascending by half steps, within a given octave. For example, starting on the open fourth string D and playing every note in between up to the next D an octave higher.

In the chromatic scale exercise, this same principle is applied to the entire range of the banjo. Starting with the open fourth string and proceeding to the highest note on the first sting, every pitch is played ascending and descending.

Left hand fingering is provided for the entire exercise.

Right hand fingering is given as a strict alternation between the thumb and index fingers. If this pattern is followed, the exercise can be played repeatedly without stopping. Again, once this right hand fingering pattern is mastered, other combinations can be used.

Special Considerations

All of the given material should be practiced slowly and precisely in the beginning. Memorization is necessary so that the focus can be solely on execution. Playing at faster tempos should only be attempted after the material is fully mastered at very slow tempos.

Emphasis should be placed on playing the material "musically". That is, to play with attention to phrasing and dynamic fluctuation to create a sense of musical expression within a given scale or exercise.

The use of a metronome is strongly recommended. Playing with a metronome instills proper rhythm and ensures precise execution. Once the material is mastered at very slow tempos, the metronome can be used as an aid in learning to play faster. By moving the metronome to faster settings in small increments, faster execution of the material can be achieved safely and systematically.

In each practice session, the fingers should be warmed up before attempting any fast or strenuous playing. A good warm up technique is to use the chromatic scale exercise found on page 29. This exercise focuses more on smooth shifting and precise finger placement rather than reaching with the fingers. Play it VERY slowly with the metronome. As the fingers on both hands warm up, then one may proceed to working with the rest of the material starting at slow tempos first.

1. Scales and Arpeggios

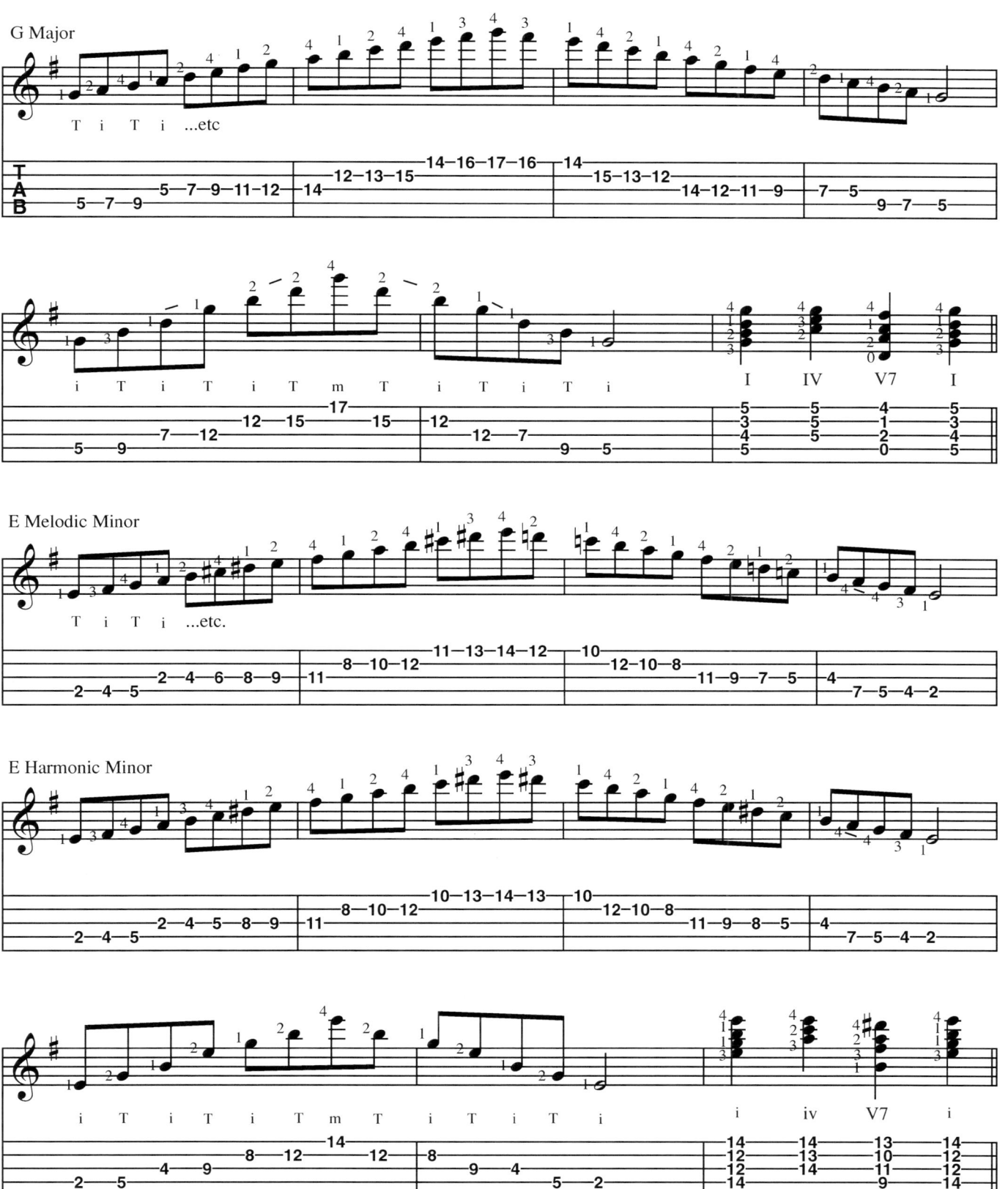

D Major

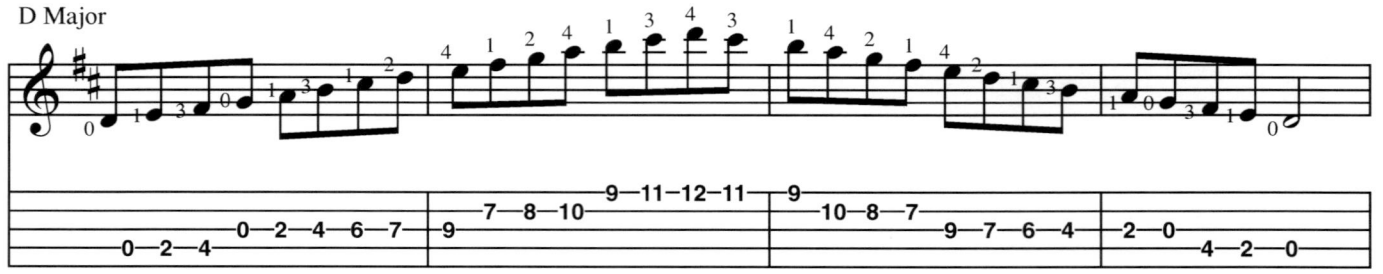

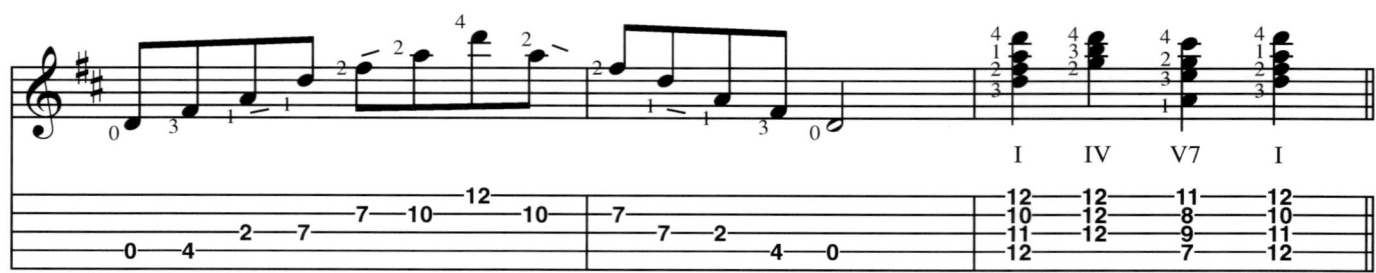

B Melodic Minor

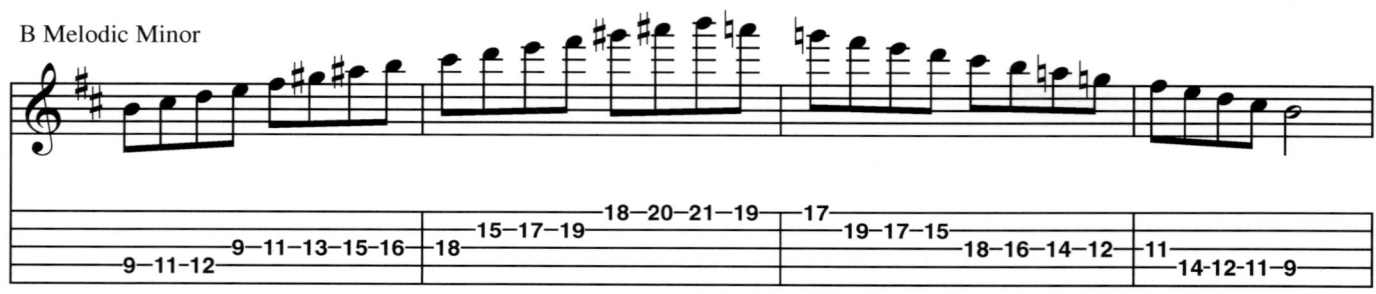

B Harmonic Minor

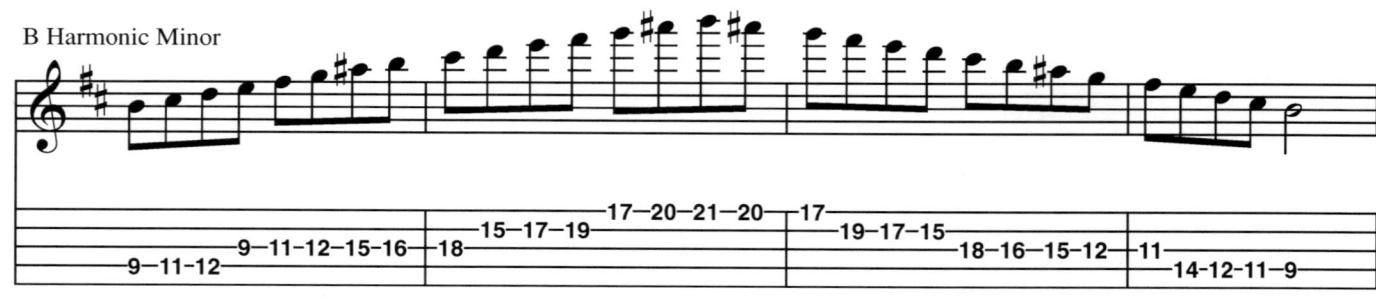

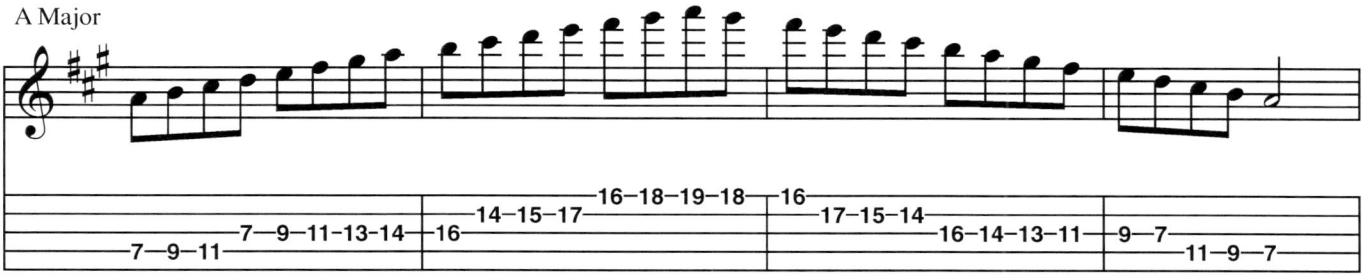

A Major

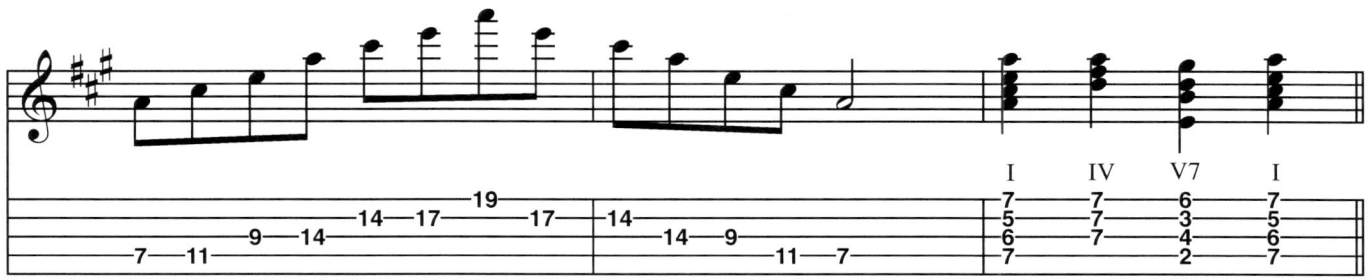

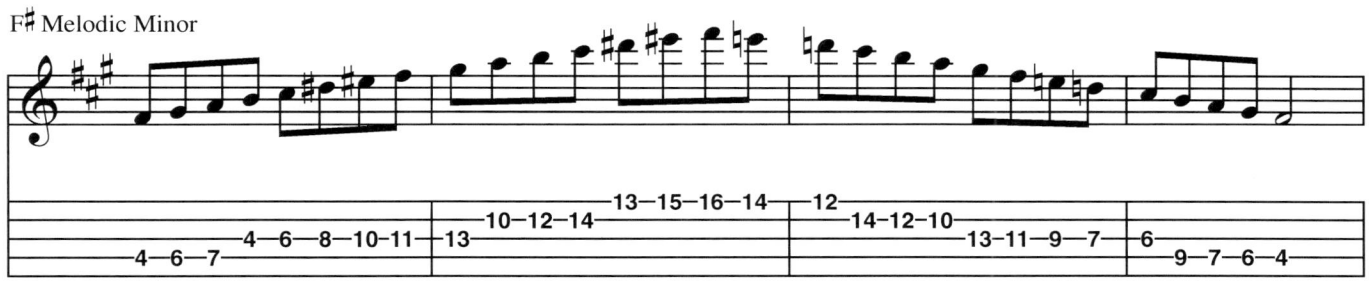

F# Melodic Minor

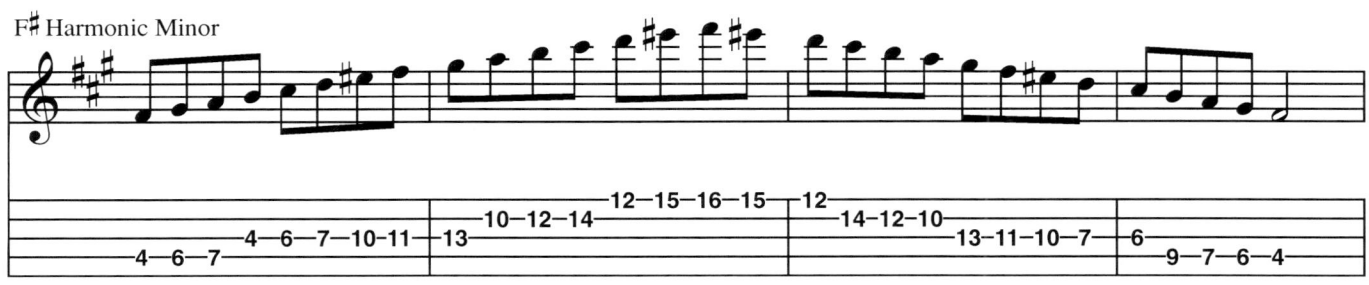

F# Harmonic Minor

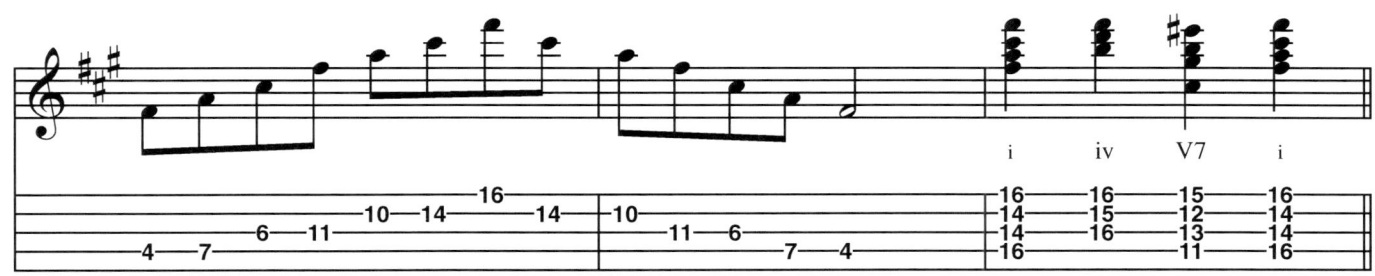

E major

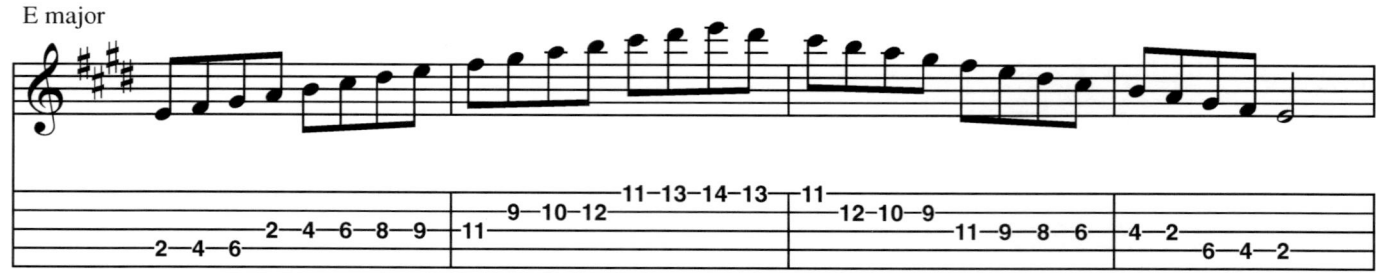

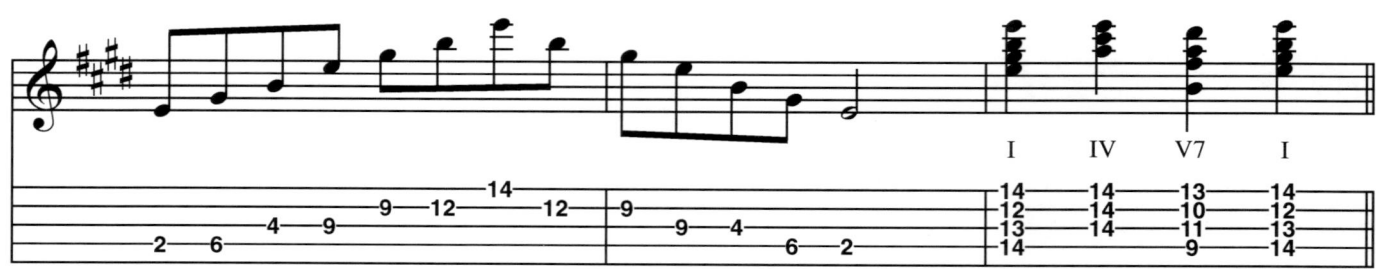

C# Melodic Minor / one octave *

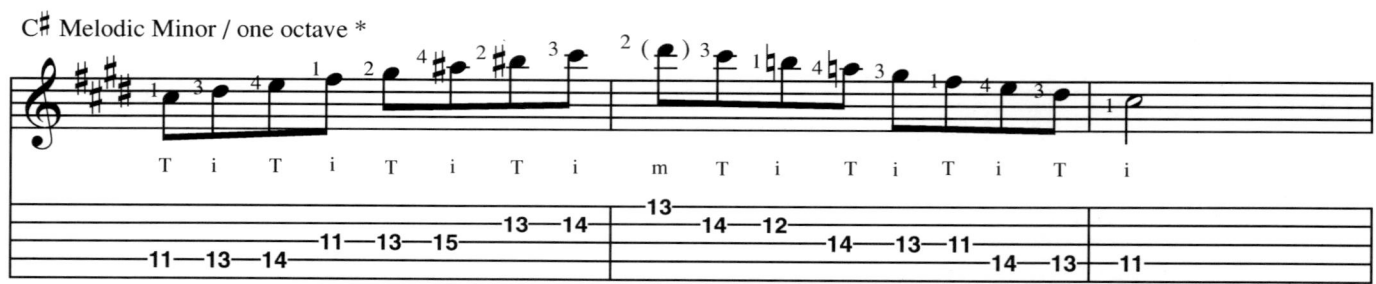

C# Harmonic Minor / one octave *

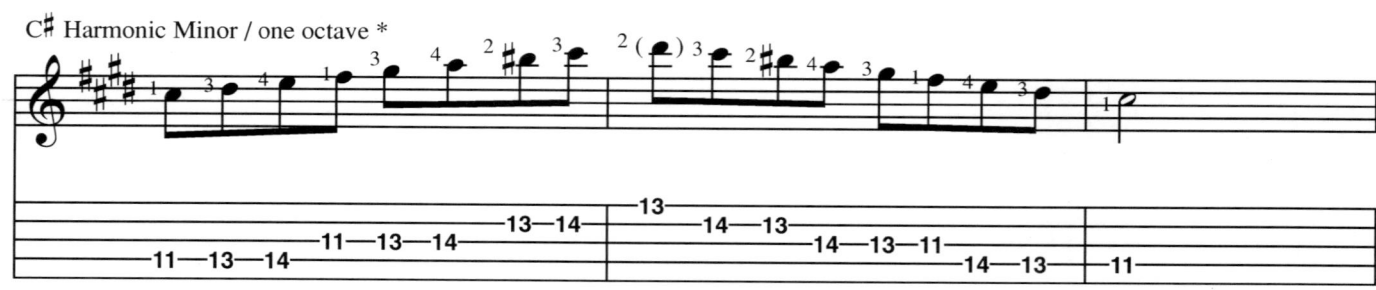

one octave*

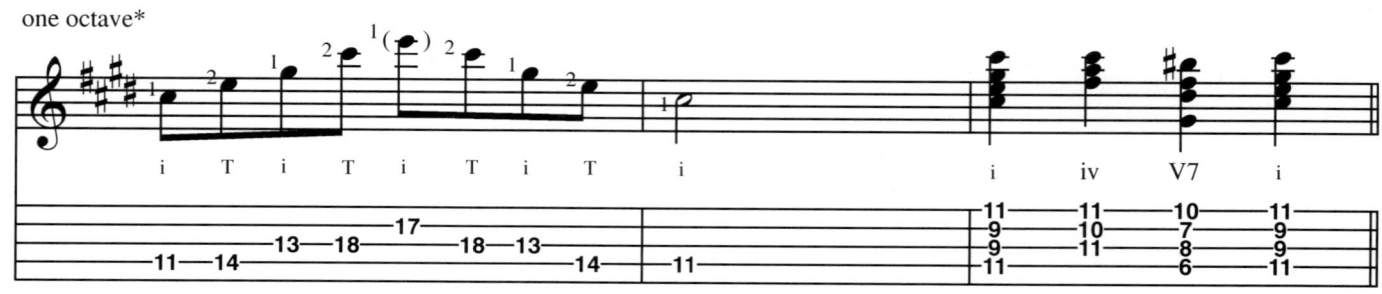

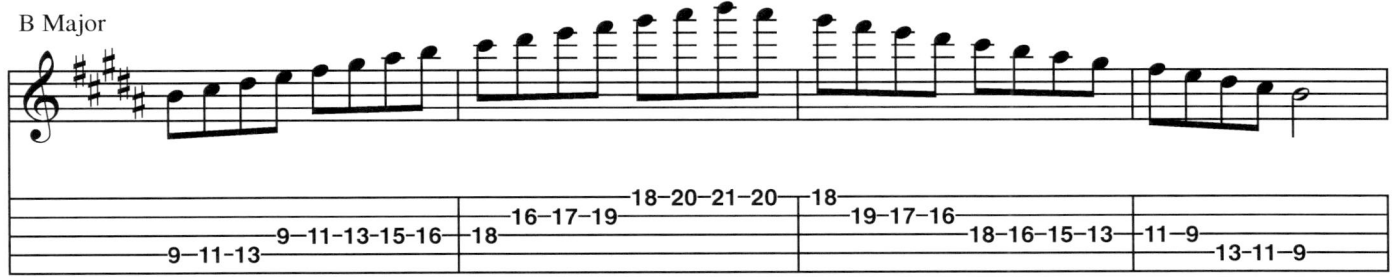

B Major

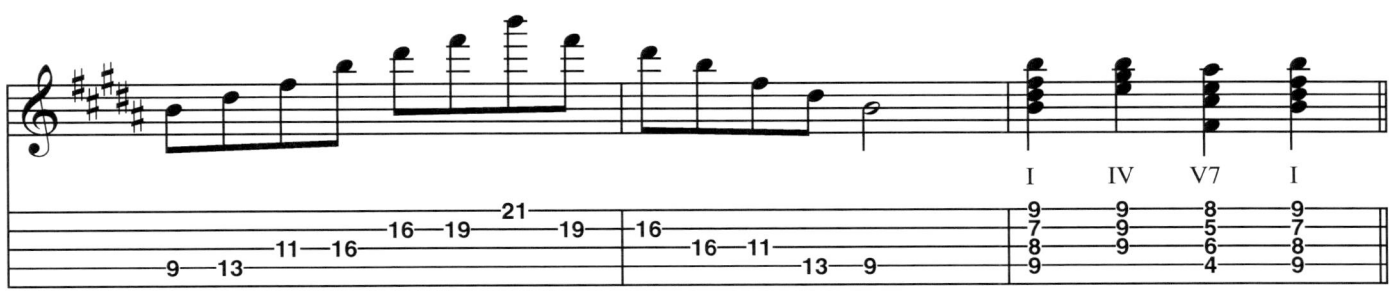

G# Melodic Minor

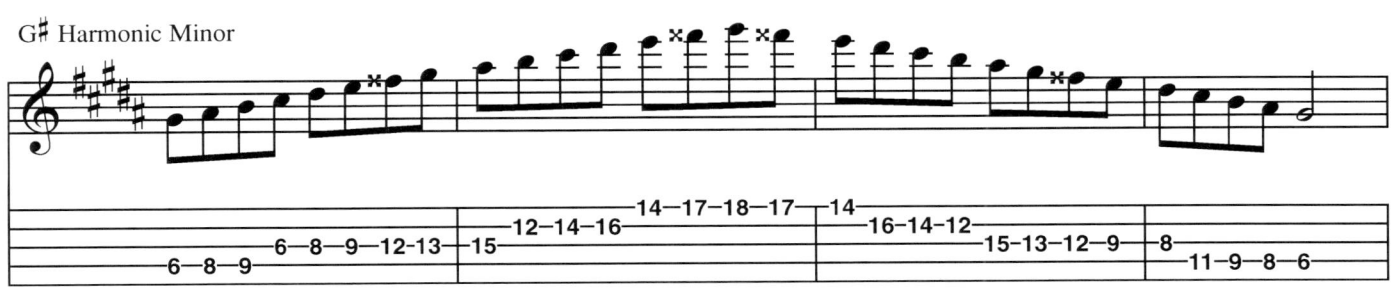

G# Harmonic Minor

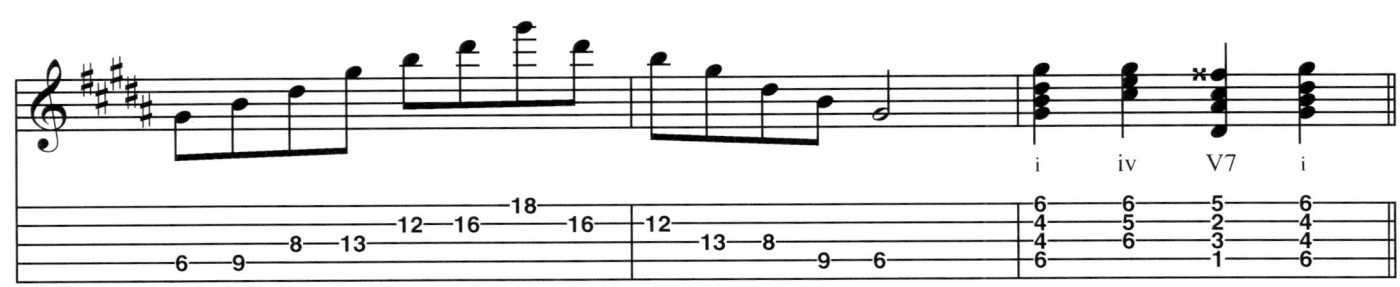

F# Major

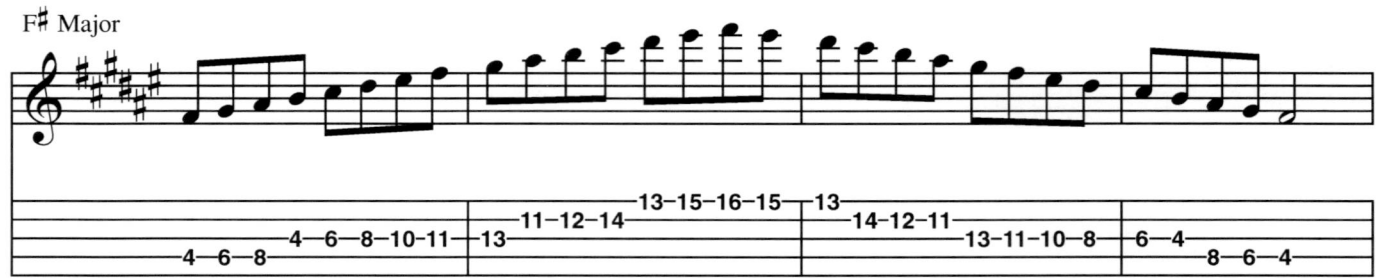
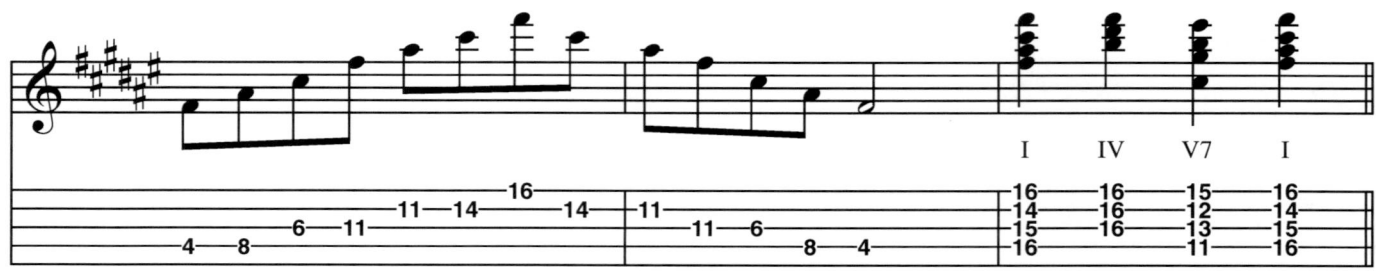

D# Melodic Minor

D# Harmonic Minor

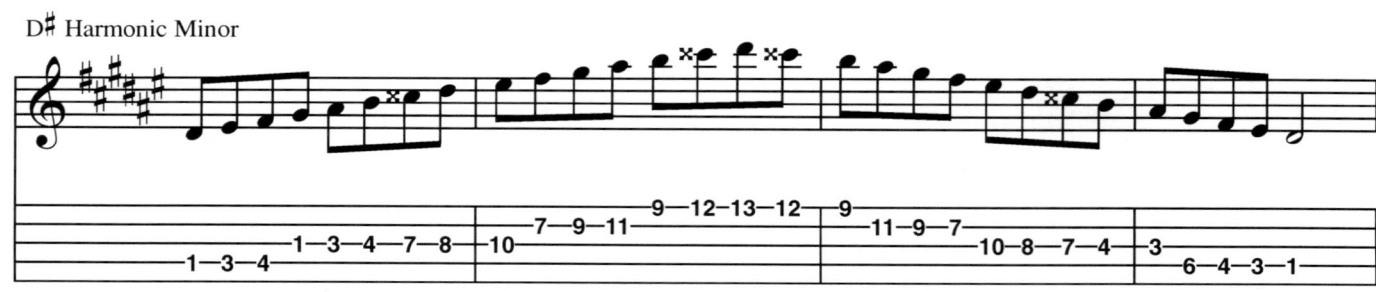
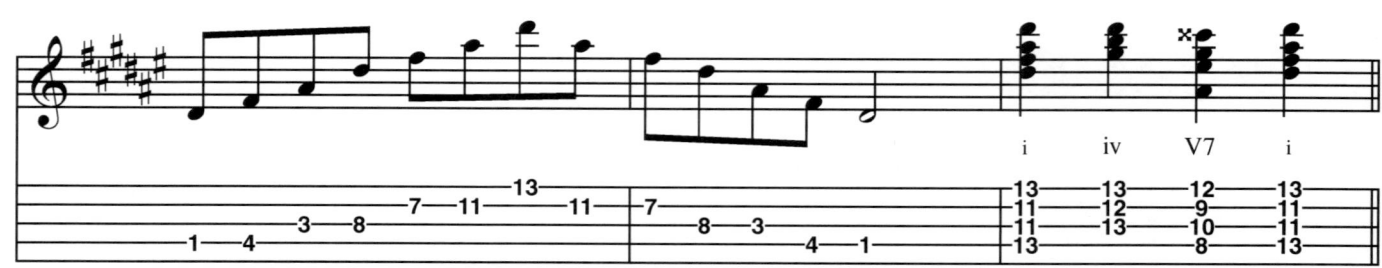

D♭ Major / one octave*

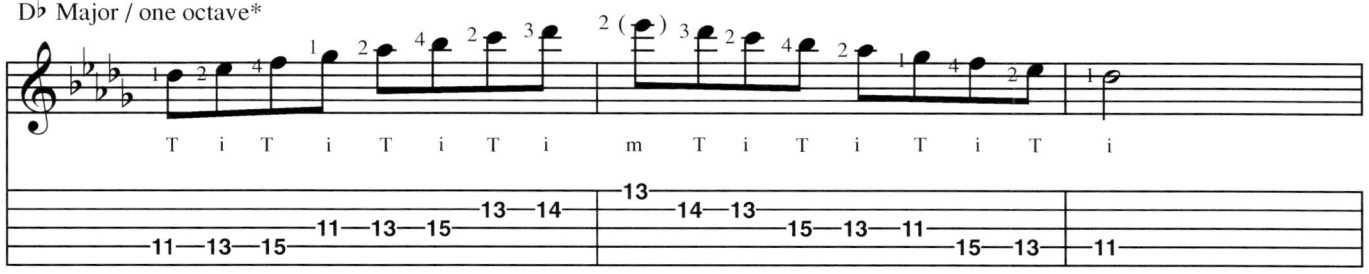

one octave*

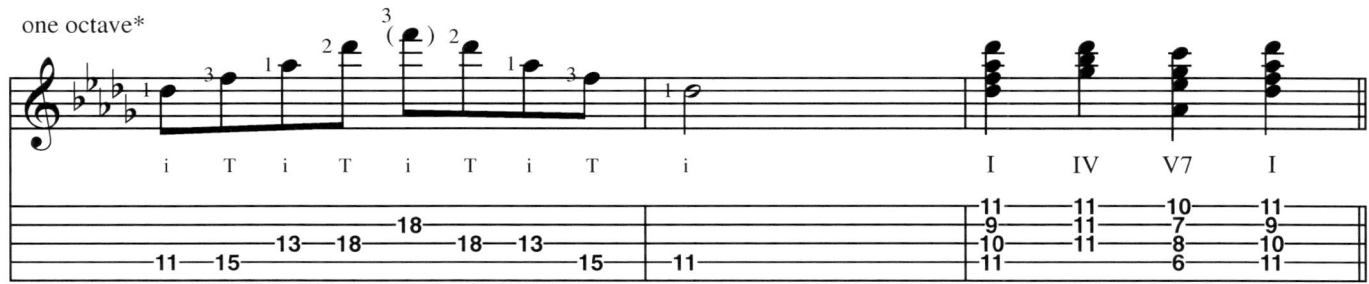

B♭ Melodic Minor

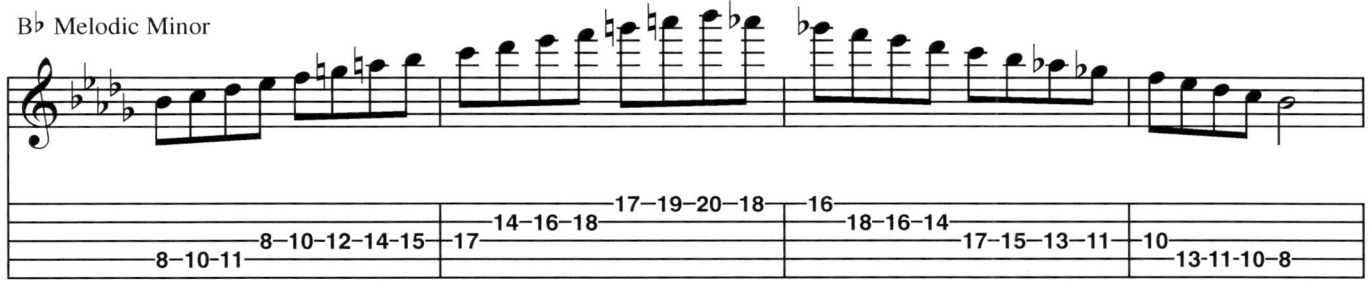

B♭ Harmonic Minor

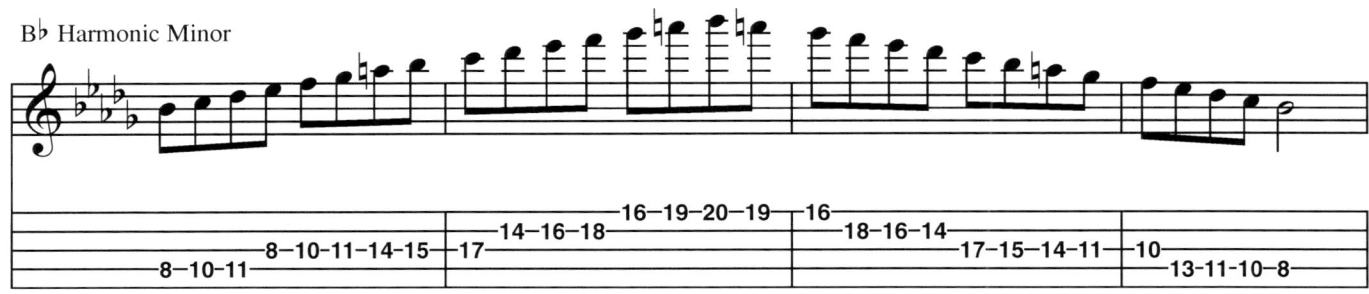

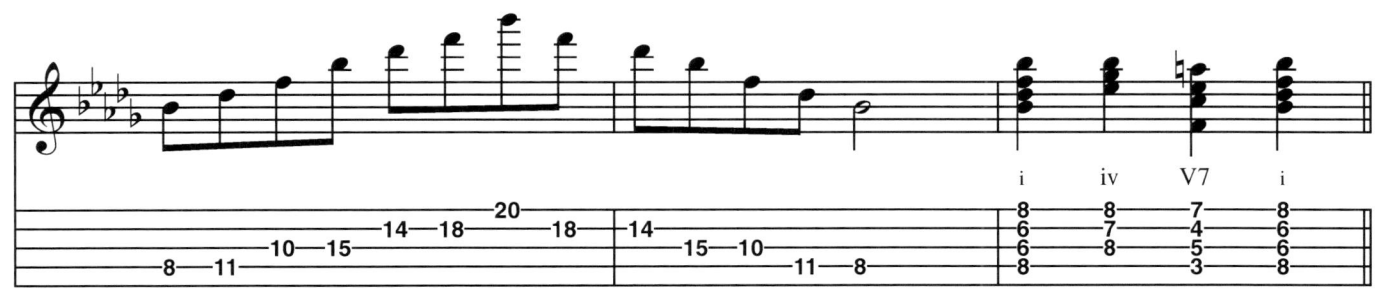

A♭ Major

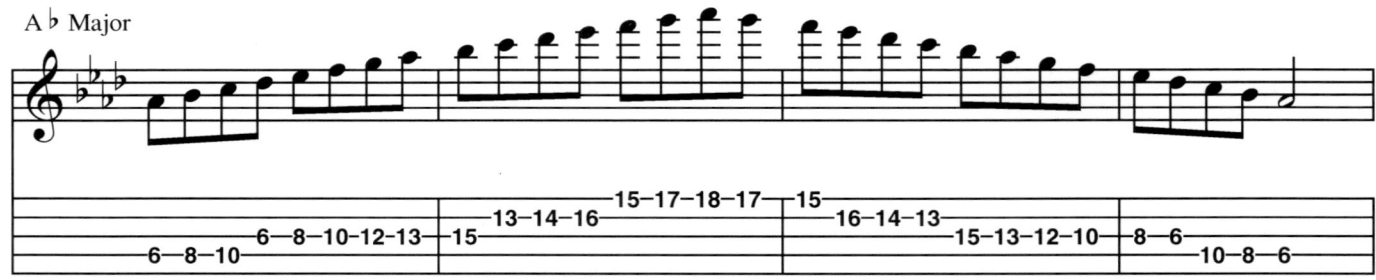

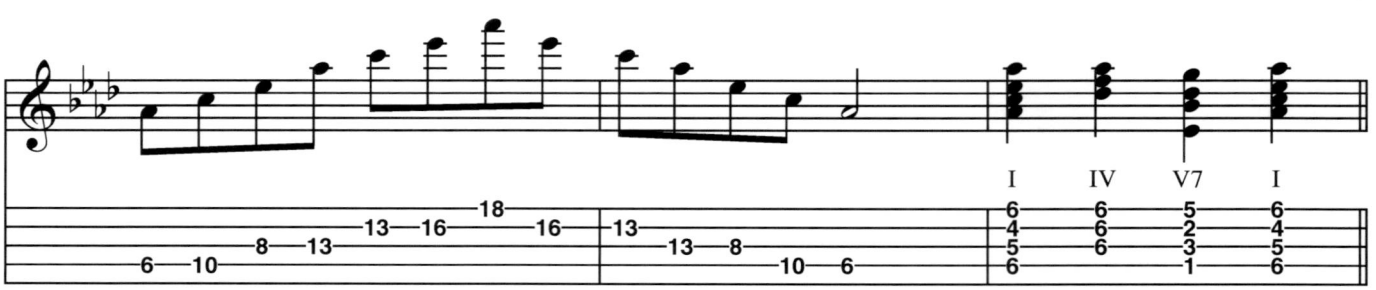

F Melodic Minor

F Harmonic Minor

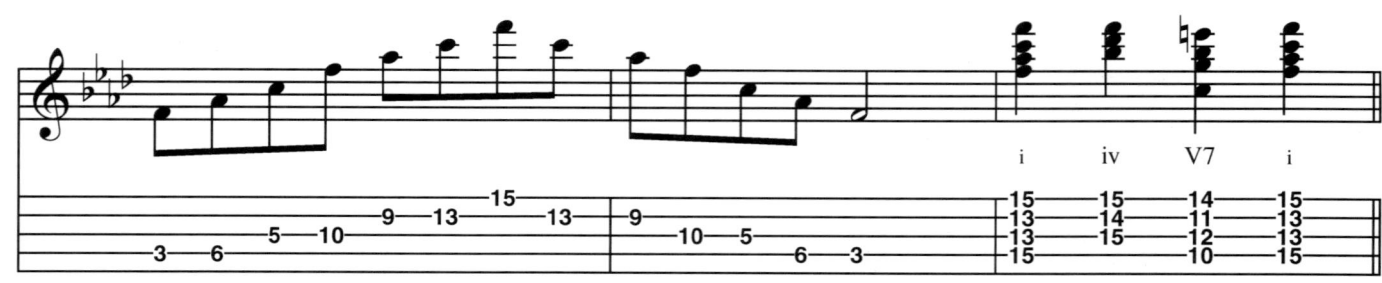

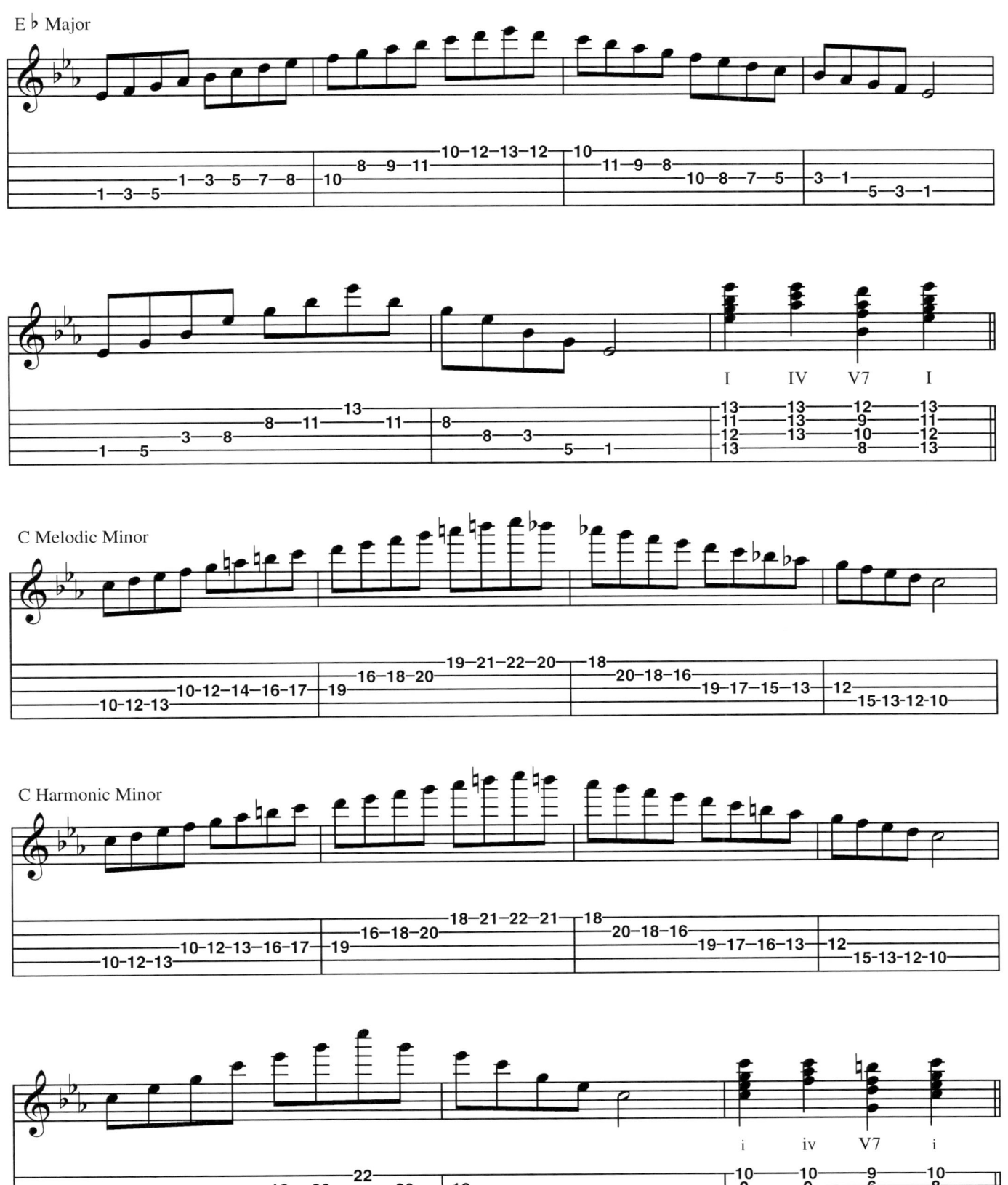

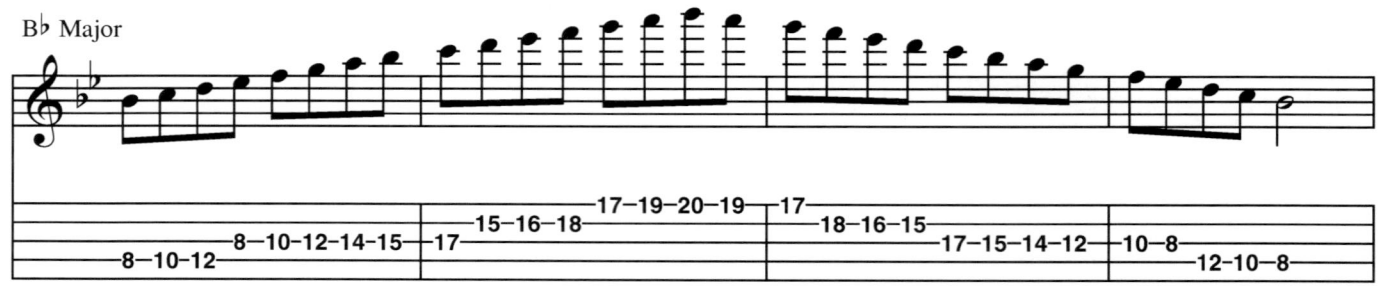
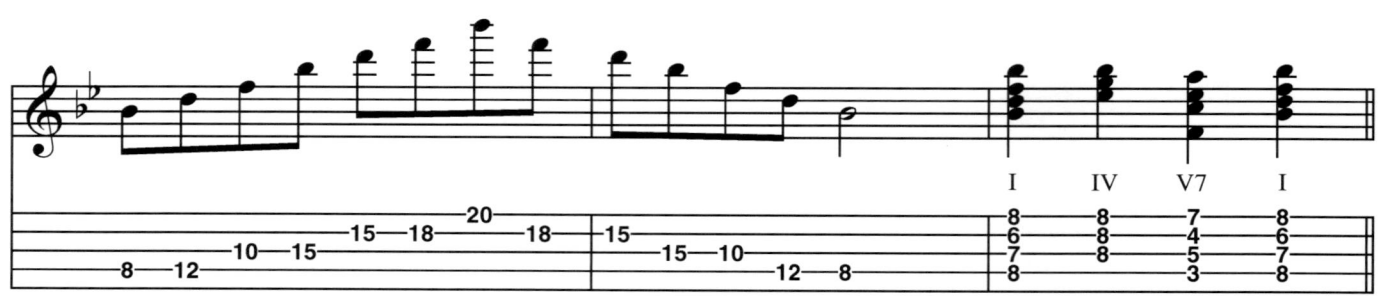

— 16 —

F Major

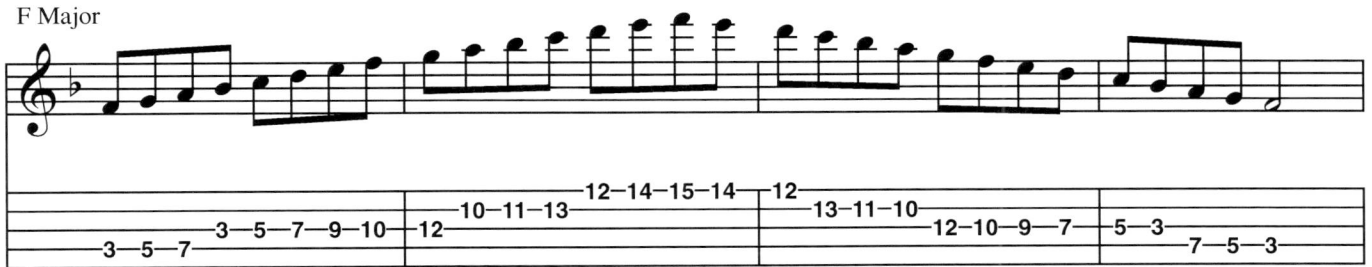
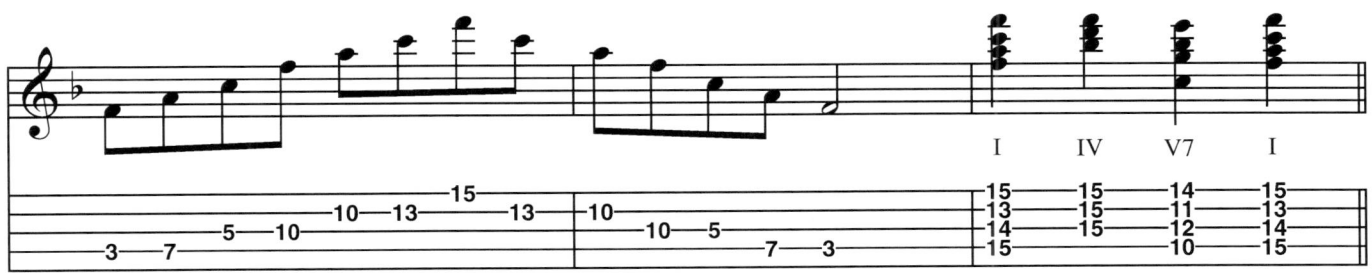

D Melodic Minor

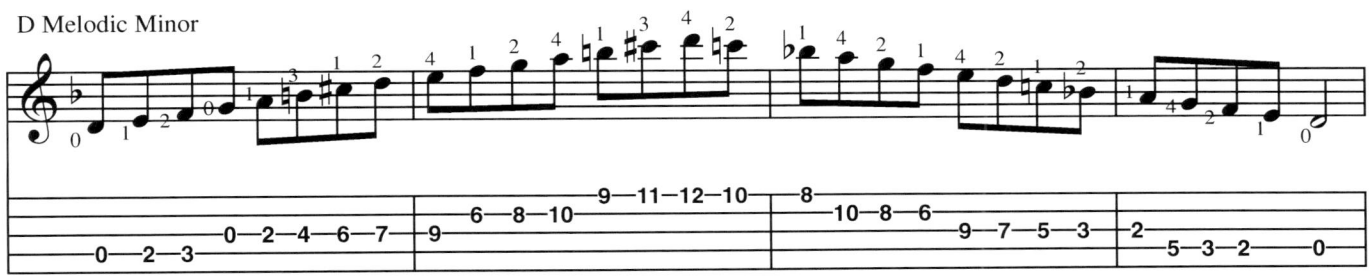

D Harmonic Minor

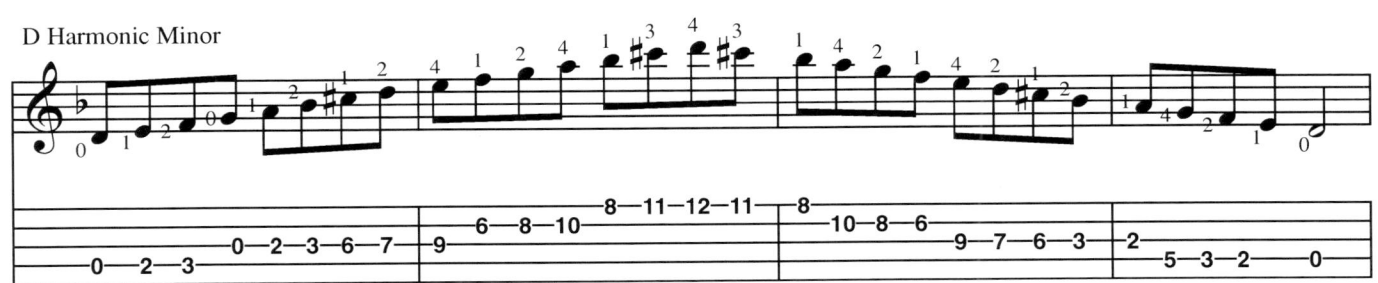
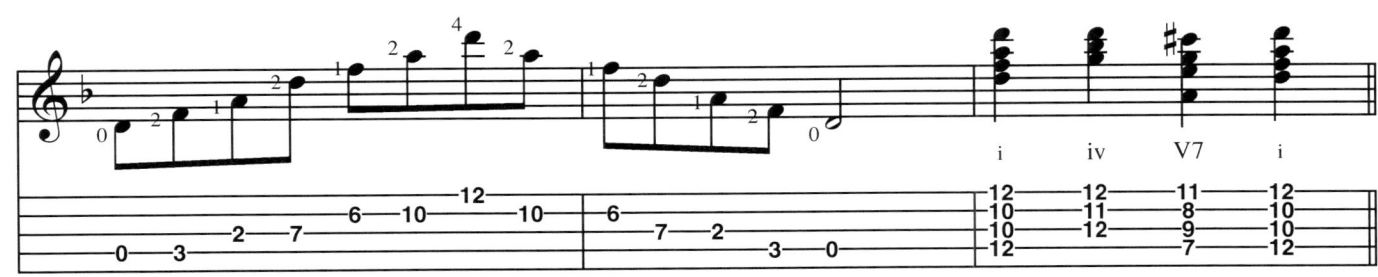

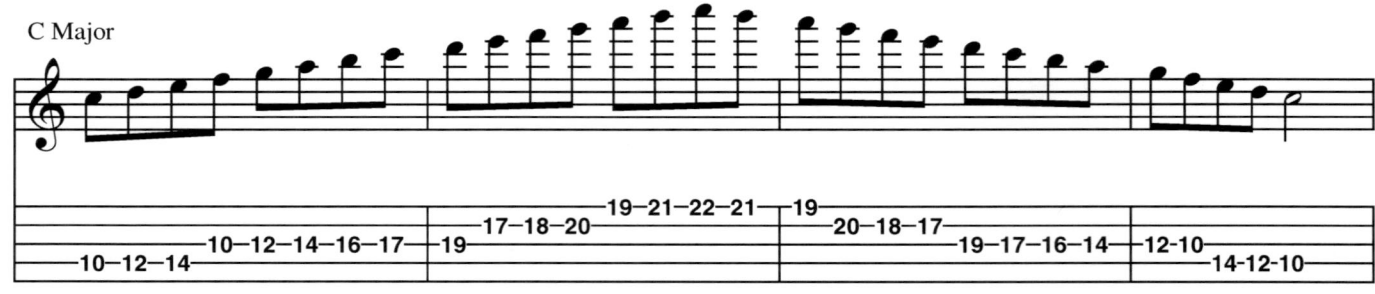

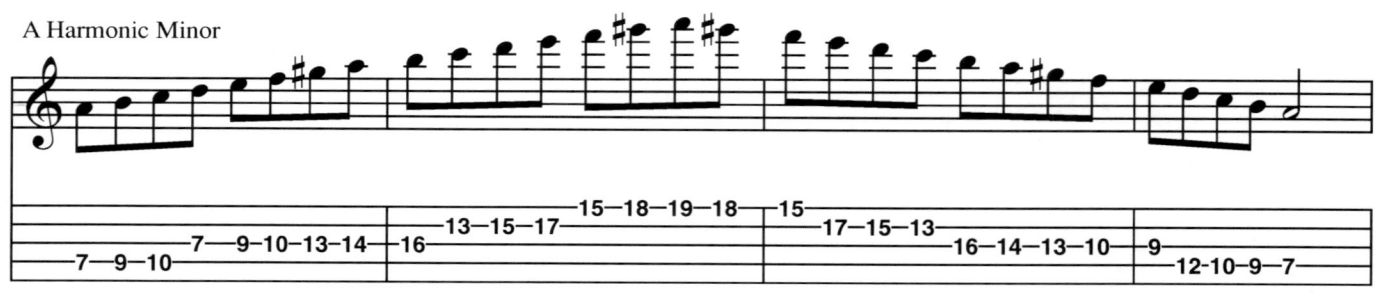
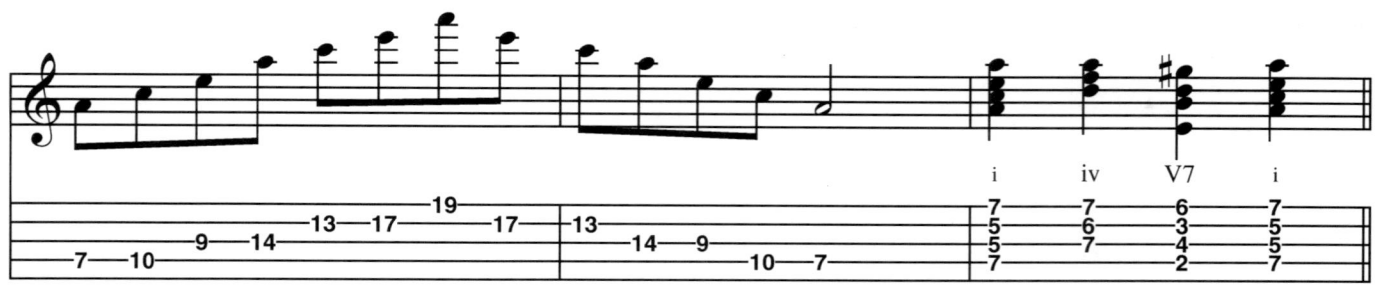

Appendix A

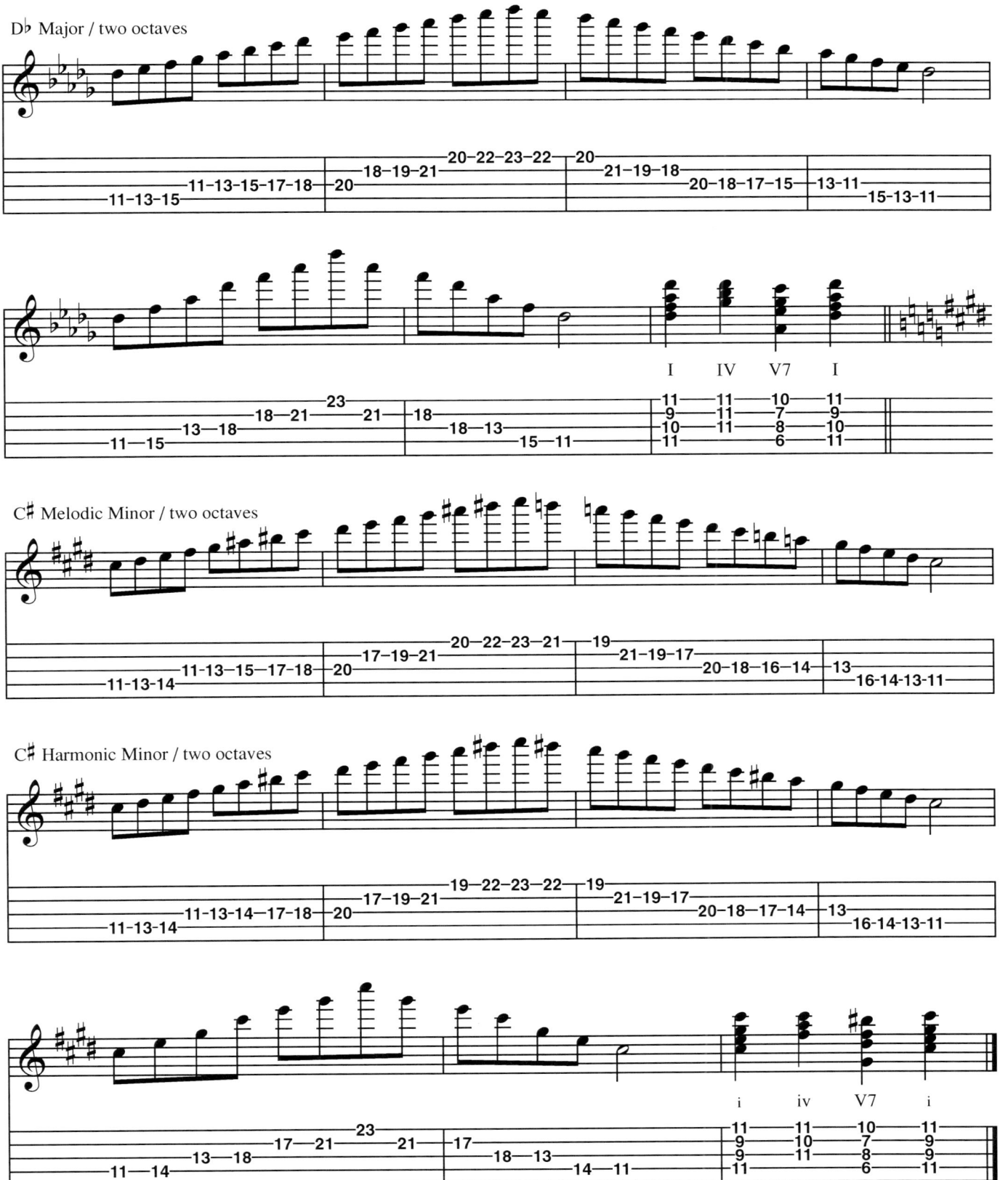

2. Continuous Exercise for Scales

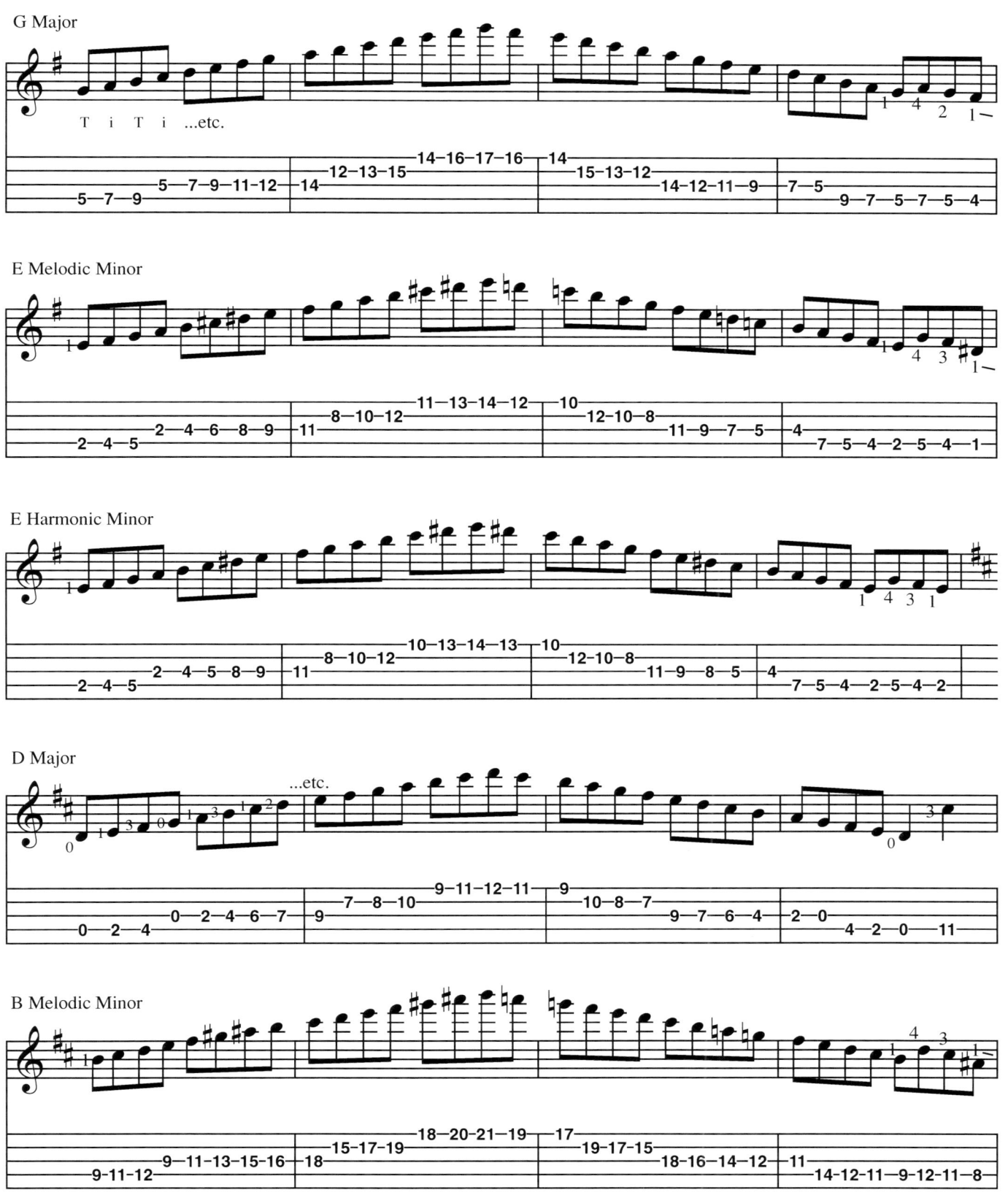

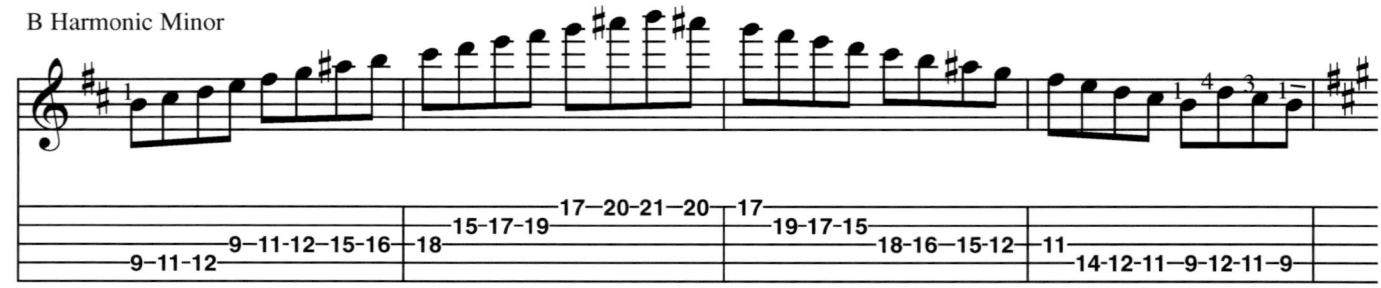
B Harmonic Minor

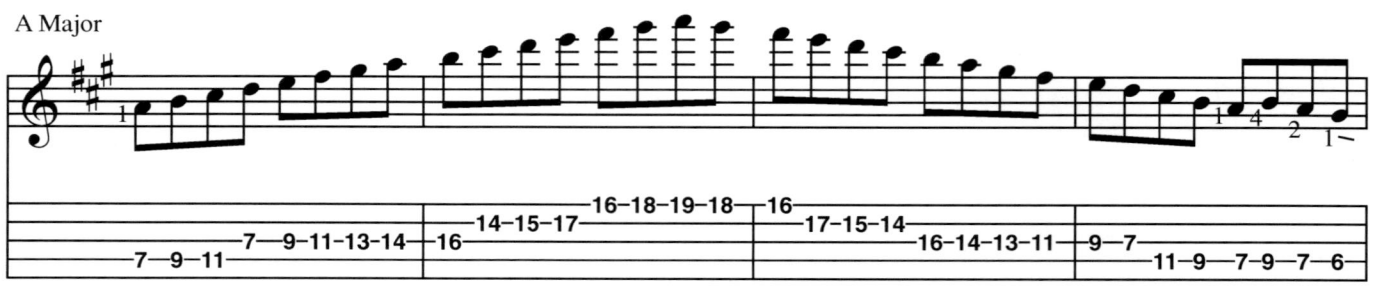
A Major

F# Melodic Minor

F# Harmonic Minor

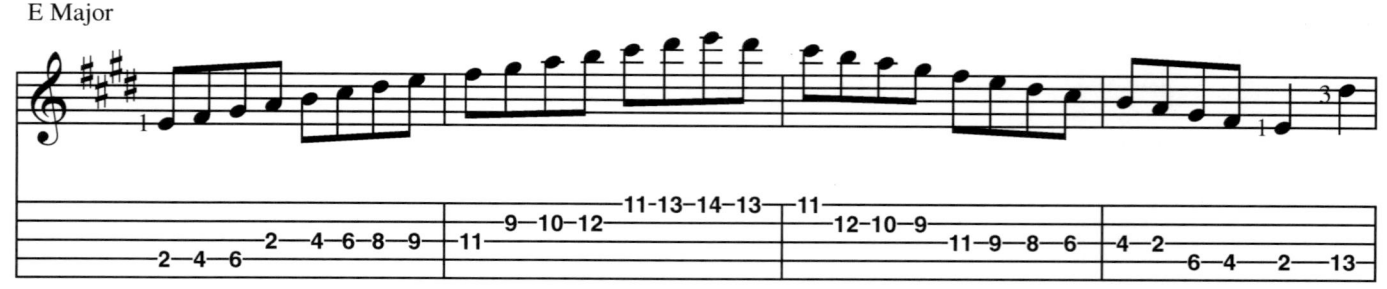
E Major

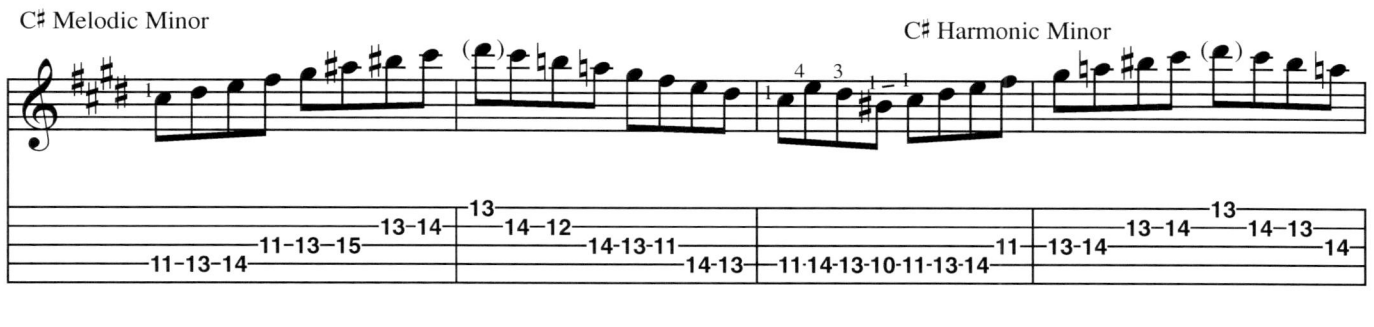
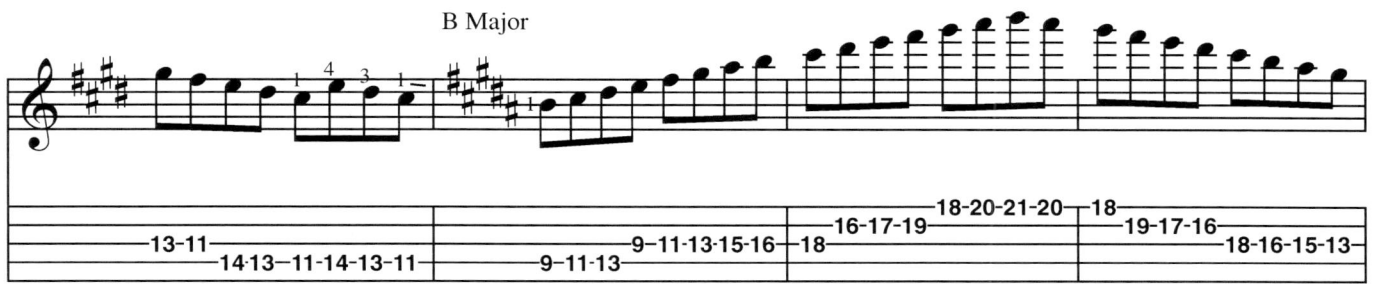
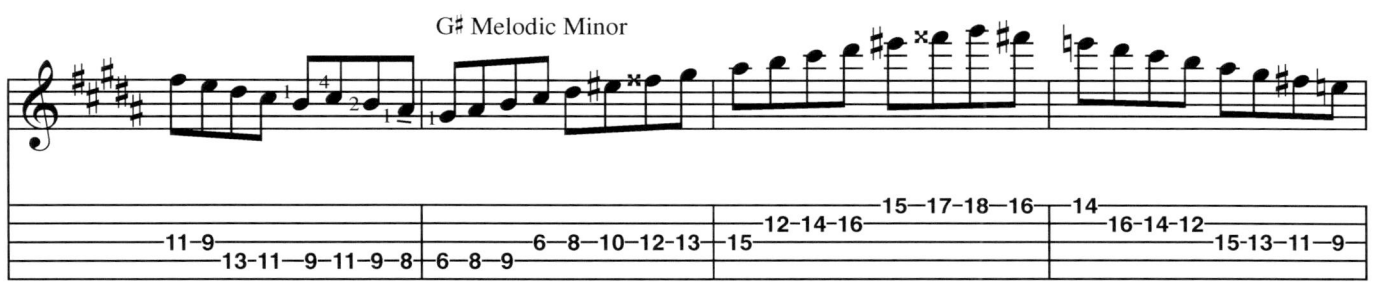
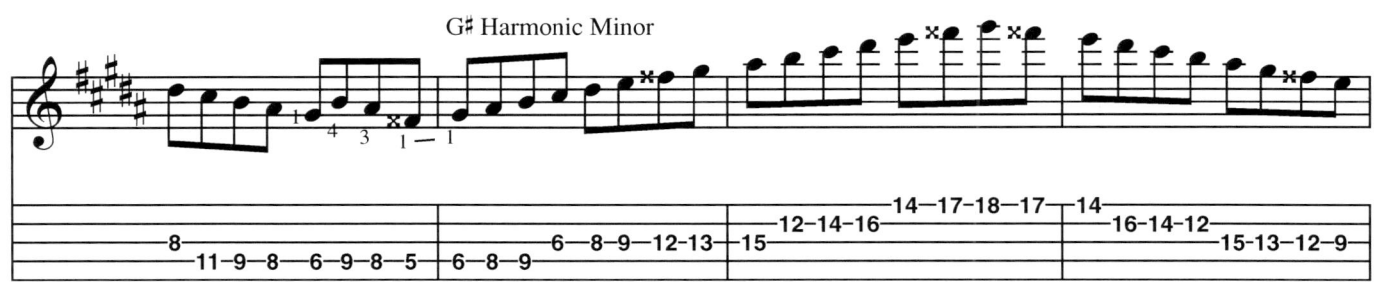
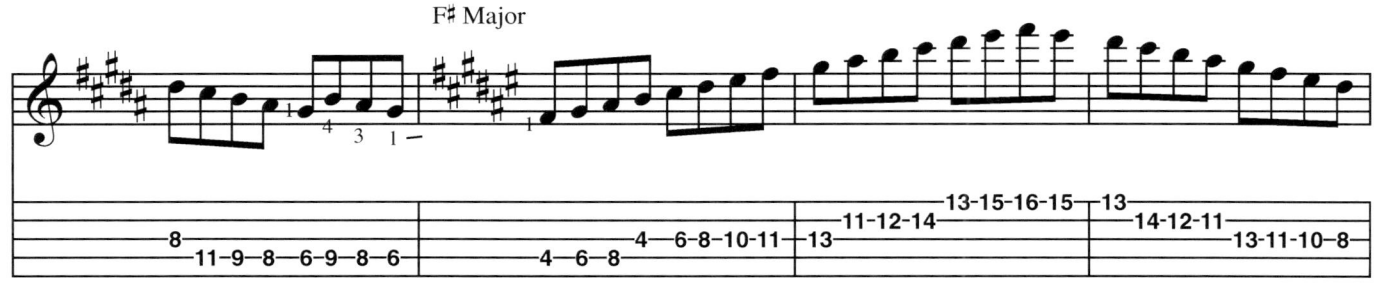

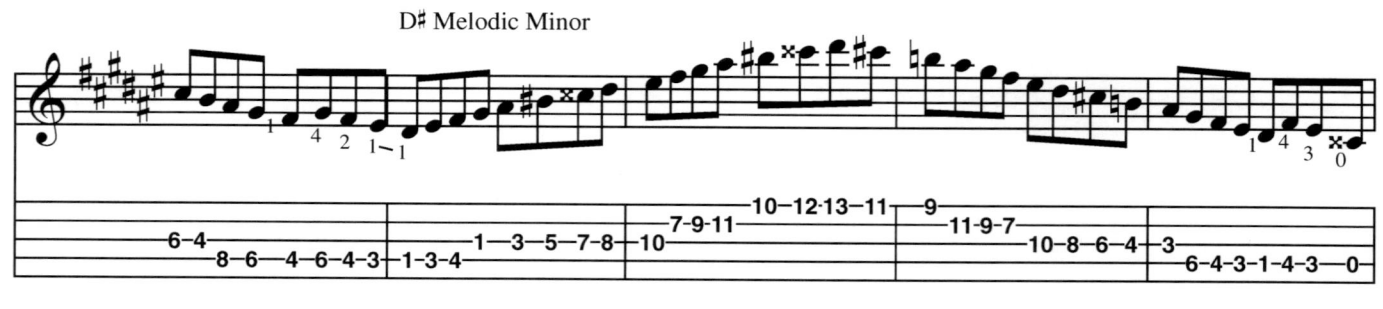
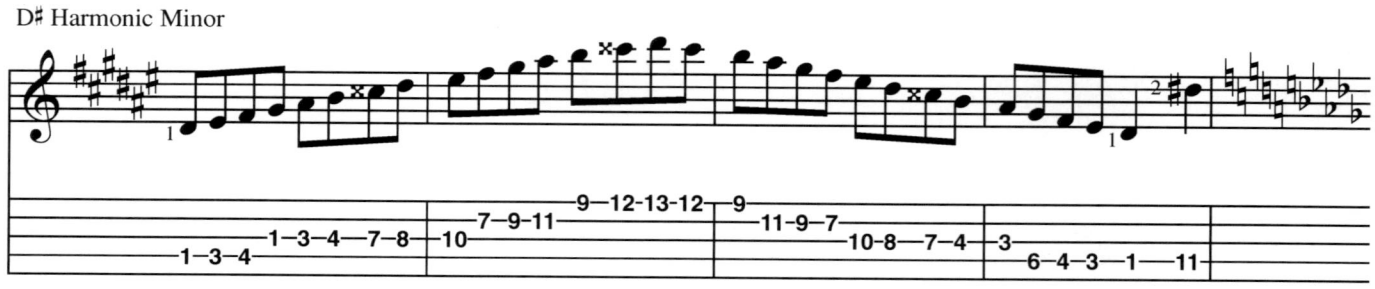

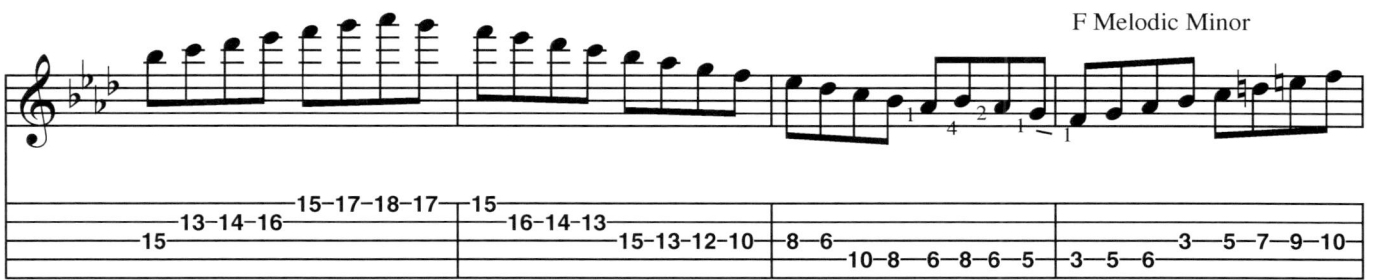

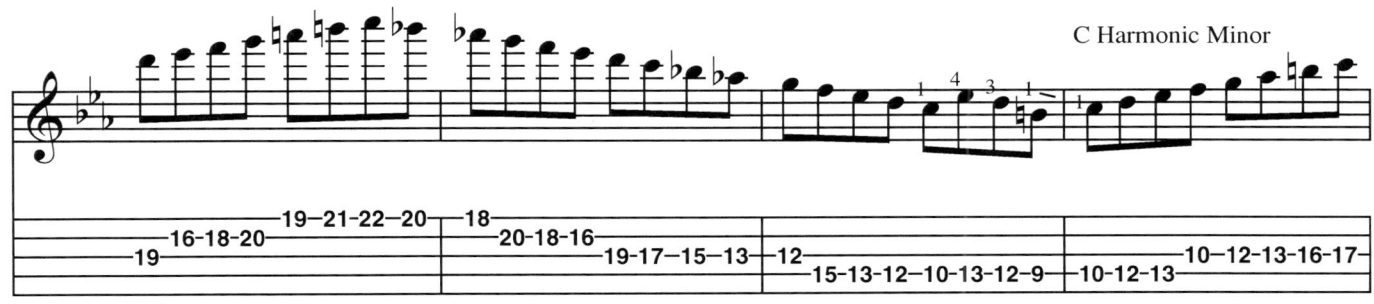

3. Continuous Exercise for Arpeggios

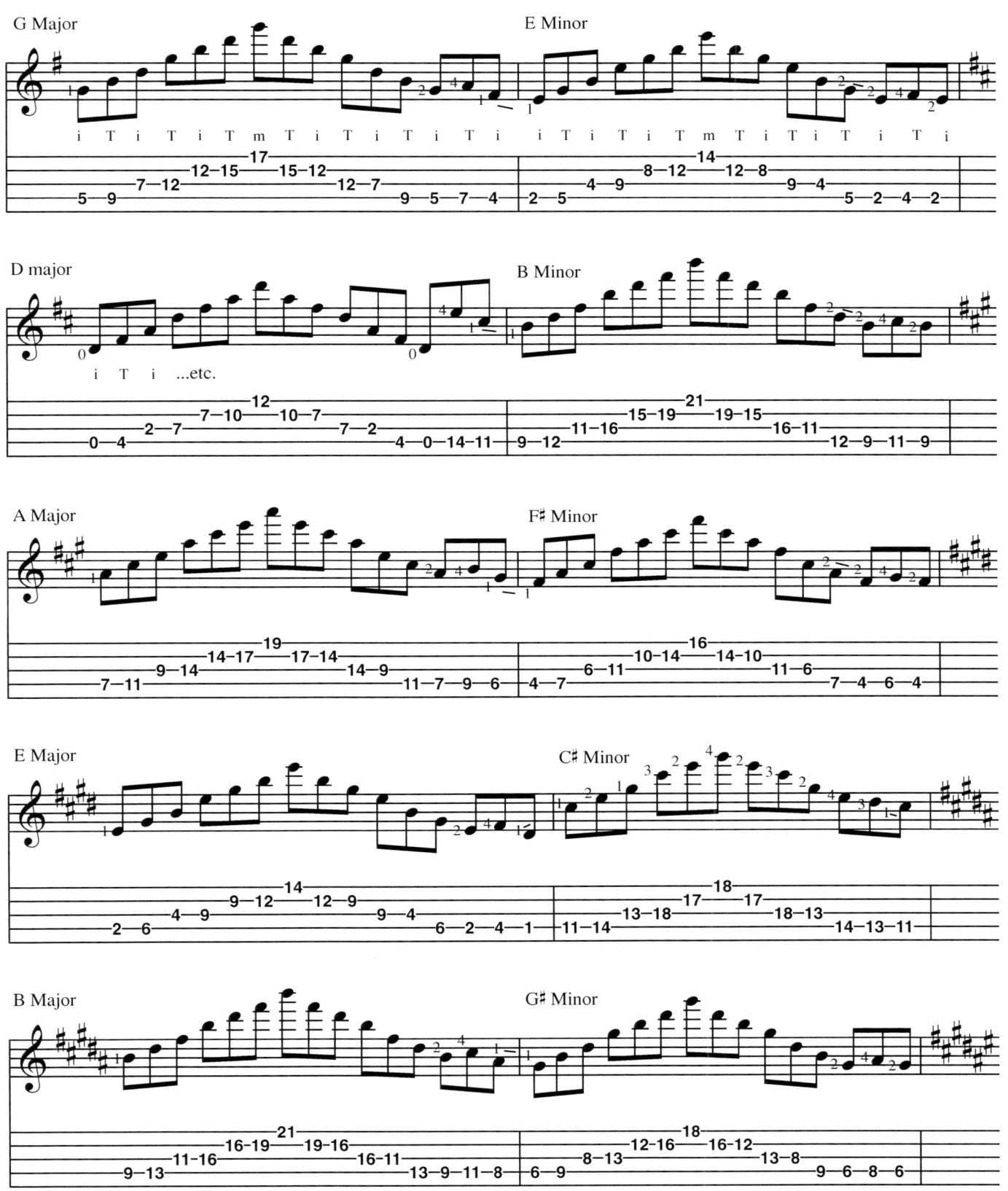

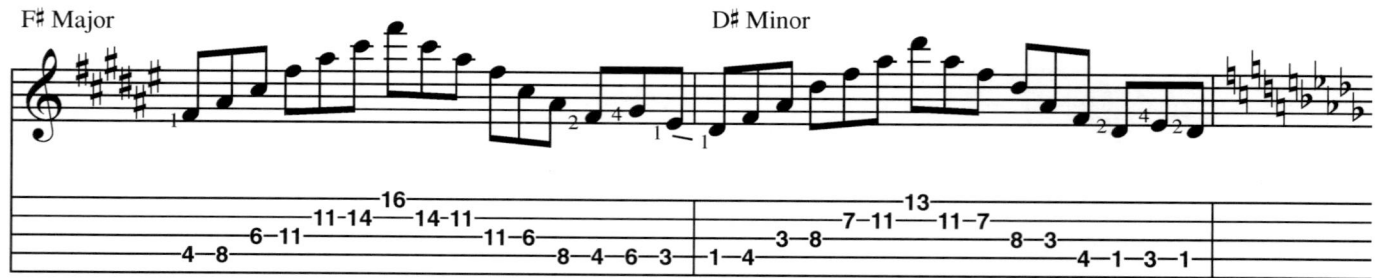
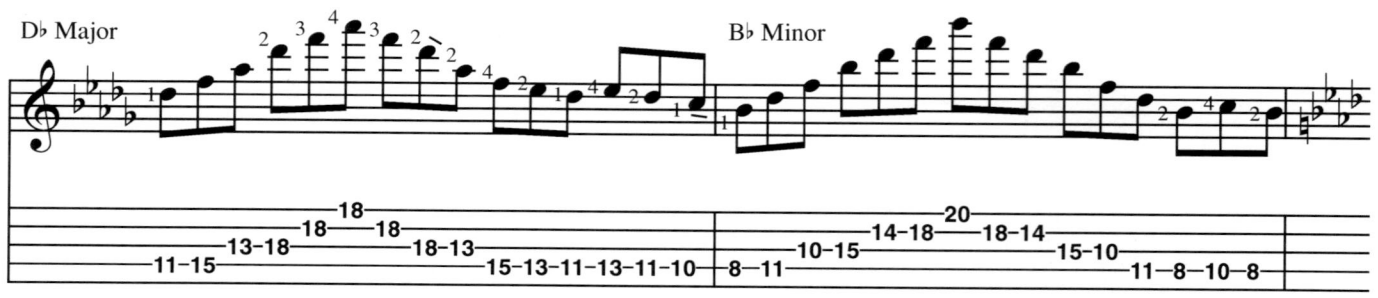
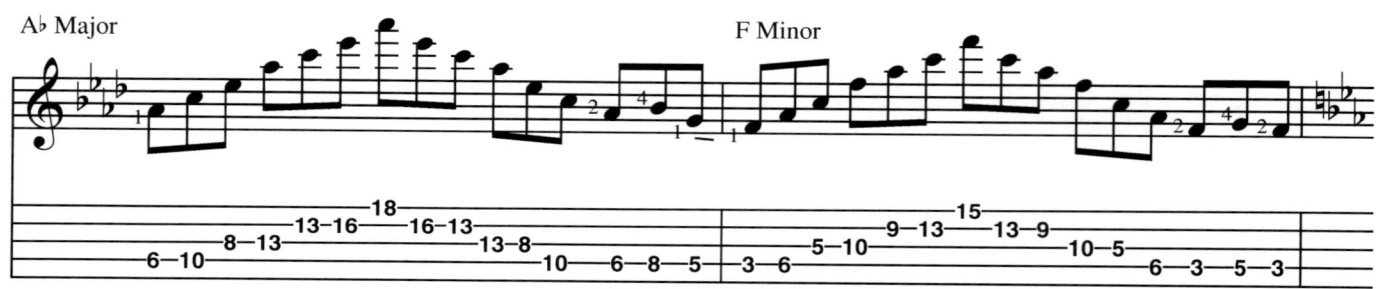
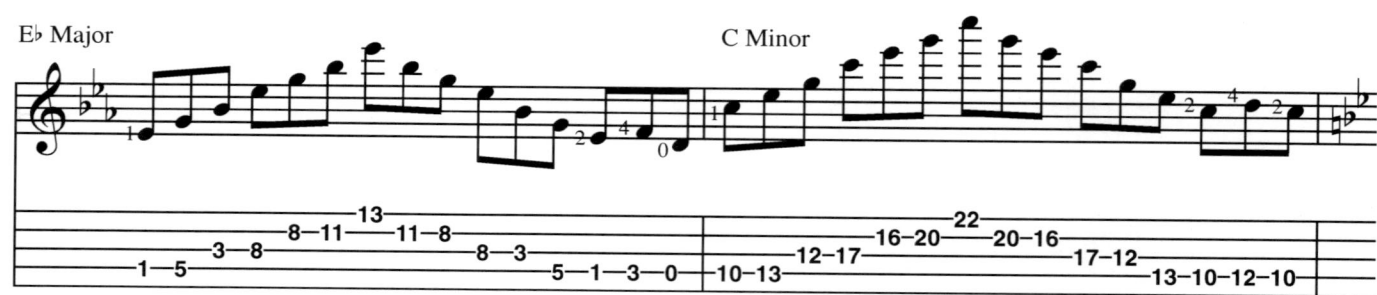
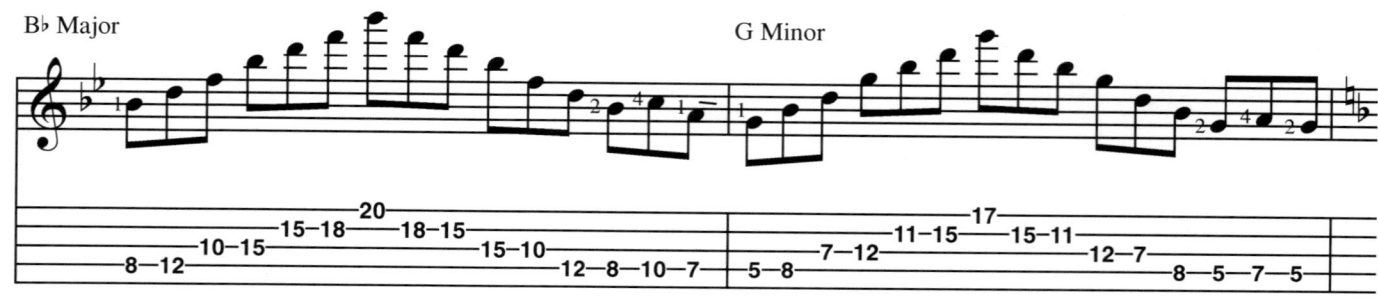

F Major

D Minor

C Major

A Minor

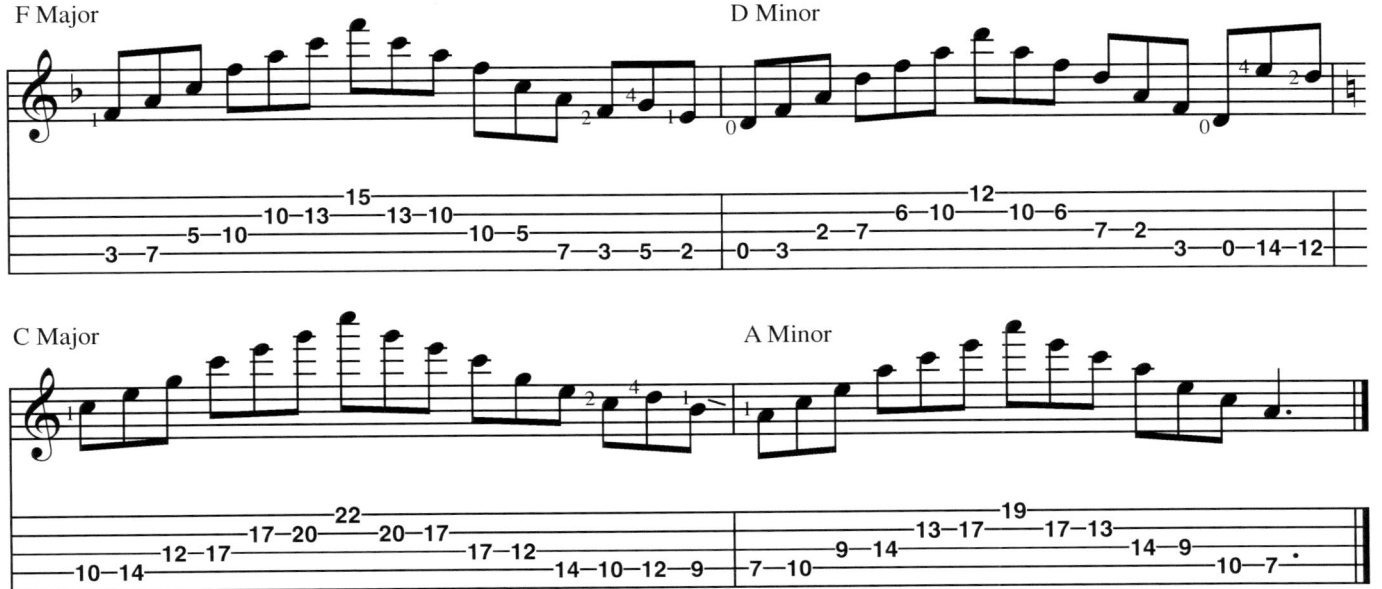

4. The Chromatic Scale Exercise

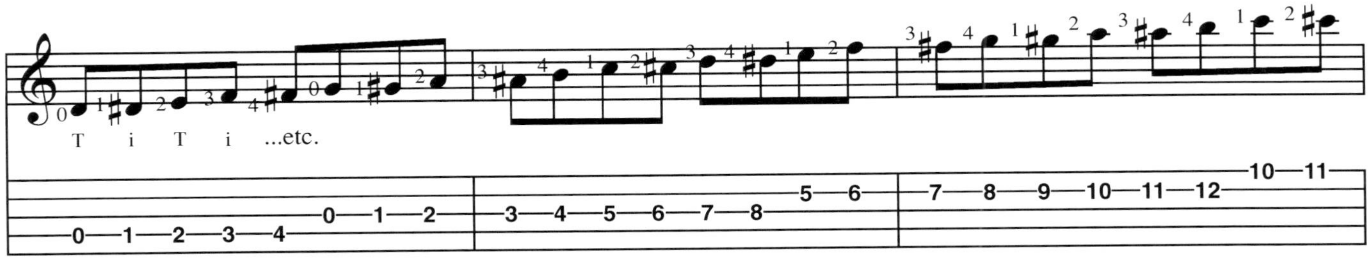

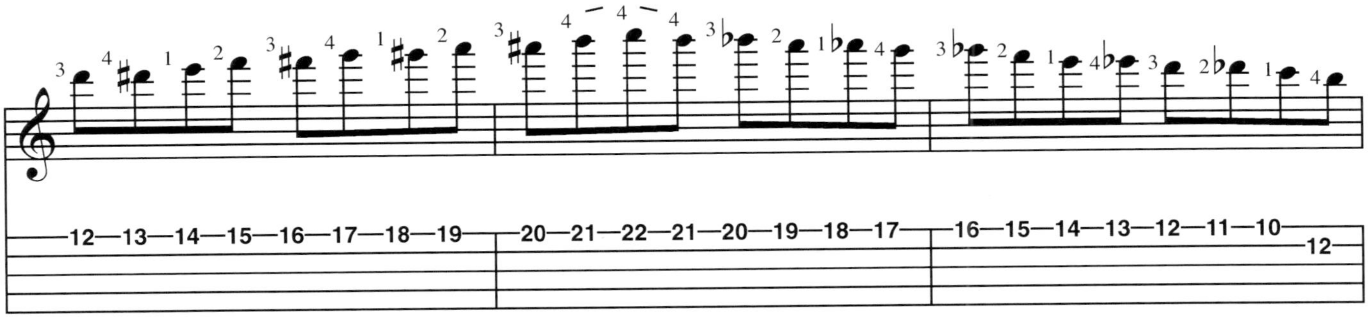

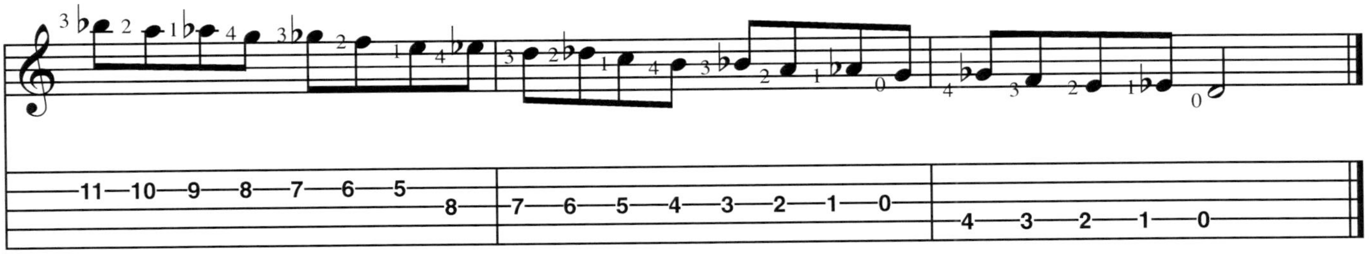

About the Author

John Bullard has attracted international attention for his work in developing and transcribing classical repertoire for the five-string banjo. His critically acclaimed CD releases include *John Bullard - The Classical Banjo* on the Dargason label and *Bach on the Banjo* on Albany Records. Mel Bay Productions published a book of his classical banjo arrangements in 1998.

His virtuoso playing was the focus of a cover story and interview in the May 1993 issue of *The Banjo Newsletter*. John, along with such luminaries as Pete Seeger and Bela Fleck, has been on the faculty of the world-renowned Tennessee Banjo Institute. He has performed throughout the United States and has been featured on numerous radio and television programs. John's classical banjo playing was highlighted in the June 2005 issue of *Vintage Guitar Magazine*.

In 2005, he became the first classical banjoist to graduate from Virginia Commonwealth University's Department of Music with a Bachelor of Music degree in Performance. Graduating magna cum laude, John was recently inducted into Pi Kappa Lambda, the prestigious national music honor society.

Two pieces from "Bach on the Banjo" are featured in the new film *The Edge of Heaven* by Turkish-German filmmaker Fatih Akin released in 2007. John's playing is included on the soundtrack recording of *The Edge of Heaven* on Essay Recordings.

In addition to his classical music, John's involvement with Bluegrass music includes work with New Appalachian Express, Virginia Rail, The Virginia Bluegrass Band, and many others.

For more information go to www.johnbullard.com